A LITTLE BOOK OF MEAT

Selima Hill was born in 1945 in London, and read Moral Sciences at Cambridge. She has spent most of her life working with children, and now lives with her family in Dorset. In 1986 she won a Cholmondeley Award; in 1988 won first prize in the Arvon/*Observer* International Poetry Competition; and in 1993 won an Arts Council Writer's Bursary. Her three previous poetry books, published by Chatto, are *Saying Hello at the Station* (1985), *My Darling Camel* (1988) and *The Accumulation of Small Acts of Kindness* (1989). She has worked on several collaborations with other artists, including *Parched Swallows* with choreographer Emilyn Claid, and *Point of Entry* with sculptor Bill Woodrow. Her fifth collection, *Trembling Hearts in the Bodies of Dogs*, is due from Bloodaxe in 1994.

Selima Hill

A LITTLE BOOK OF MEAT

BLOODAXE BOOKS

ISBN: 1 85224 243 4

First published 1993 by
Bloodaxe Books Ltd,
P.O. Box 1SN,
Newcastle upon Tyne NE99 1SN.

Bloodaxe Books Ltd acknowledges
the financial assistance of Northern Arts.

Cover printing by J. Thomson Colour Printers Ltd, Glasgow.

Printed in Great Britain by
Bell & Bain Limited, Glasgow, Scotland.

'If you need to ask, you'll never know'
REGINA CLINE O'CONNOR
to her daughter Flannery O'Connor

Acknowledgements

If I thought she would have liked it, I would have dedicated this book to my late mother. As it is, I dedicate it to Laura Gilmore, with apologies for failing to use her title *Les Vaches Mystiques of the USA* which I record here now as an alternative. Thank you.

I would also like to thank the late Thomas Merton and his friends and correspondents Thich Nhat Hanh and Flannery O'Connor. Their books include: THOMAS MERTON: *The Seven Storey Mountain*; THICH NHAT HANH: *The Sun My Heart*; FLANNERY O'CONNOR: *Wise Blood* and *A Good Man is Hard to Find*.

I am grateful, too, to Sally Fitzgerald for her edition of Flannery O'Connor's letters, *The Habit of Being* (Farrar, Straus & Giroux, 1979), from which the first three lines of the poem 'Daily Prudence' have been taken. Also to Beat Sterchi and his translator Michael Hofmann for *Blösch* (Faber, 1988). And to Sujata Bhatt, especially for her poem 'What Is Worth Knowing' in her collection *Brunizem* (Carcanet, 1988). I would like to think that some readers of my book will turn to the works of these authors too, and be inspired by them, as I have been.

And I would like to thank Bluebell, my grandmother's cow, and Birdie, my faithful dog, both currently uneaten.

I would also like to thank the School of English and American Studies at the University of East Anglia for awarding me a Writing Fellowship in 1991.

Acknowledgements and thanks are also due to the editors of the following publications in which some of these poems first appeared: *Ambit*, Bernard Samuels' Rimbaud Festival programme at Plymouth Arts Centre, *The Honest Ulsterman*, *London Magazine*, *London Review of Books*, *The New British Poetry* (Paladin, 1988), *The New Poetry* (Bloodaxe Books, 1993), *New Statesman & Society*, *Poetry Book Society Anthology 1989-1990* and *The Poetry Book Society Anthology 3* (PBS/Hutchinson, 1989 and 1992), *Resurgence*, and *Writing Women*.

Finally, I would like to thank Xavier Lambours for permission to use his photograph, *L'Oeil d'un Bœuf*, on the front cover.

Contents

Lust

Lust's the answer – lust
like pessaries
that glide along my veins;
like gilded lozenges.

Beyond the dunes,
where soldiers eat soft chocolate,
palaces are falling.
Lust's the answer.

Little Sisters

Up to their angelic necks in steers and guinea fowl,
there are girls growing up into women
without knowing why;
there are duck-feeding mothers
and duck-feeding, stern-faced daughters,
their dresses smelling of church
and giant azaleas,
who haven't the slightest idea
what they've got coming to them;
who toil away,
gingerbread-mixing,
geranium-nursing,
fancy-breed-raising,
permanent-waving,
inspired by the jelly-eating Sisters of St Joseph of Corondolet,
by the Little Sisters of the Poor, whom no one knows,
by little angels –
daughters who think they understand everything,
who practise fudge- and crystallized-violet-giving,
who breed glum swans,
and wobbly spotted mules,
for whom the only males are bulls and cobs,
and the only man they know is the Man they don't,
Who might appear out of the woods at any moment,
with blood on His hands like a sunset,
and somehow redeem them;
whose private lives are disturbed
by the sound of a van
with somebody nobody's asked for, or wants, at the wheel.

Auction Day

While I was quietly doing nothing all day
but feeding the geese their stale corn-kernels
and manicuring the Guernseys
in preparation for the Registered-Guernsey-Cow Auction-Day,
something irresistible
lurched into my life,
something unknown, from nowhere, with eyes like Alaska,
and growls,
and sighs,
and offers of what it proclaims will be Permanent Joy
in exchange for a home,
in exchange for a home with me.
So what am I supposed to do, Our Lady
– casserole it?
What am I supposed to do I want to know.

Our Lady of Meat

Our Lady of Meat,
Our Lady of goose,
Our Lady of pain;
Our Lady of lips,
Our Lady of nipples,
Our Lady of jelly;
Our Lady of house-coats,
Our Lady of wedding-dresses,
Our Lady of sweet peas;
Our Lady of Calomel,
Our Lady of vans,
Our Lady of jam;
Our Lady of casseroles,
Our Lady of corn-kernels,
Our Lady of Virginity, and Renunciation, and resisting things;
Our Lady of nothing,
Our Lady of never,
Our Lady of Love –
what am I supposed to do I'd like to know?

Don't Let's Talk About Being in Love

Don't let's talk about being in love, OK?
– about *me* being in love, in fact, OK?
about your bloated face, like a magnolia;
about marsupials,
whose little blunted pouches
I'd like to crawl inside, lips first;
about the crashing of a million waterfalls
– as if LOVE were a dome of glass beneath a lake
entered through a maze of dripping tunnels
I hoped and prayed I'd never be found inside.

At night I dream that your bedroom's crammed with ducks.
You smell of mashed-up meal and scrambled egg.
Some of the ducks are broody, and won't stand up.
And I dream of the fingers of your various wives
reaching into your private parts like beaks.
And you're lying across the bed like a man shouldn't be.
And I'm startled awake by the sound of creaking glass
as if the whole affair's about to collapse
and water come pouring in with a rush of fishes
going *slurpetty-slurpetty-slurp* with their low-slung mouths.

The Devastation of Easter Island

I don't know if you've ever
waited for someone to smile at you,
but if you have, you'll know how I'm feeling now:
all the other smiles for all the other people
fall and melt
like snow from another age
forming rivers where beautiful women are walking
down avenues of trees into the sea;
but all I want
is for *you* to smile at *me*.

I don't know if you've ever
wanted someone to stretch out their hand and touch you,
someone who's been sitting beside you all afternoon
like an uninhabited stone
and driving you mad;
or like a ceremonial stone fish-hook
you're desperate, you're praying, to be fished by –
but if you have,
you'll know how I'm feeling now.

You're numb as hair,
as mute as cats,
as soft as lettuces,
as resolute and mysterious
as the cause of the devastation of Easter Island
where nothing remains except heads,
and a few long-legged chickens
that don't mind drinking sea-water.

I don't know if you've ever
done nothing all day but *languish*,
but if you have, you'll know how I'm feeling now.

Sleepless Nights

Because you scream like a sluice,
because you scream like someone waking up at night
with raging toothache,
like a cargo of half-wrapped lorries
being unloaded into some remote terminal
with lots of shouting and gesticulation;
like the Mongolian Empire itself,
thundering with obese horesemen;
because the last night I spent longing for you
was like spending the night with no clothes on
in a Daimler full of chows
with the windows closed,
I have decided to calm myself down,
and imagine my head as a tinkly moss-padded cavern
where nothing happens.

Ignore Me

Ignore me.
I went to sleep last night quite normally,
but in the morning I was someone else, not me –
someone who's been wallowing in dreams of you
like pea-hens in a stranger's flower-beds;
who's heavy with desire
like sacks of meat;

who gets to her feet, crashes about
like a two-legged escaped rhinoceros
in pursuit of anyone who looks remotely,
or sounds remotely, or smells remotely,
like you – then mumbles forlornly *I'm sorry*.
I'm sorry.
Ignore me.

How Many Men

How many men are as mysterious
as a clipped crop circle in a spinach field
in San Soupplets in 1963;
or fingerprints on vomit
the police can't dust?

as cold as frozen bananas
sannyasins at Poona eat,
still hard, so they eat less banana;
as pained-looking as a flayed rider;
as improbable a partner
to a humble peacock-raiser like myself
as owning one's own golf-course
to a worm;

as eerie as a tunnel
barges have to go through
with the help of leggers
lying on their backs in the darkness,
while the horses walk above them in the light?

how many other men
are as unapproachable as a phalanx of fork-lift trucks by day,
and about as easy not to think about at bedtime
as milk-chocolate milk,

or as someone who might possibly –
if I was the luckiest person in the world,
which I'm not,
and won't ever be
(and I mind very much that I won't be) –
treat me like *a loved one,*
besides you?

You, my hero-shaped hero,
you, my indifferent bear.

I Think About You All the Time

I think about you all the time. I think:
that you live in a world of meals cooked by cooks;

that someone like me's quite wrong for someone like you;
that I owe my energy to the squashed pituitary glands

of thousands of little pigs butchered daily
at the Armour Packing Plant in Chicago, Illinois.

And in my dreams you're giving me Chicago.
And in my dreams I'm resurrecting pigs.

North Carolina

Everything about you's a bit like me –
in the same way that North Carolina's a bit like Ribena
but rhymes with Vagina, which is nearly the same,
but much darker –
brutal and sweet like disease,
sweet as an asphalt dealer.

Imagine a cloud.
Imagine eating a cloud.
Imagine your mouth being full of the cloud like the world.
And imagine a person like me with a person like you.
I have turned you into a cloud.
Prepare to be eaten.

The Longing of the Meat Trade

The longing of the meat trade
for dead pets,

of icy waters
for the lost Titanic;

the longing of a stadium
for heroes

is like a whim
compared to mine for you.

Speak To Me

I'm going to stop.
I'm going to start again.
I'm going to make strategic little piles
of things like cigarettes and sugar-cubes,
and bantams' eggs, and cubes of cattle-cake,
and range them, along your route,

until you notice them;
and then I'm going to balance
slightly larger things,
like fish, or fruit, or tulips, on my head,
whispering as I walk: *Speak to me*;
whispering *Speak to me please.*

The Airport

You whisper
like a palm cupping egg;
like a dish of bruised celery hearts
spooned from a tin
whose label we don't understand the language of,
or the country even;

like firs beyond the parking lot at 4 a.m;
or the youngest milker, all dressed in white,
or the youngest handler.

But I want you to talk, talk, talk.
I want you to talk so much
eternity with all its glittering and rattling stars
and moons like clocks would not be long enough to hear you out.

But you're talking like a little worm in trousers;
you're talking like a fish in a bonnet;
an unforgivable slug in something being passed off as a side-salad.
Be fat.
Be warm.
Be Matisse in Tahiti.
Imagine aircraft soaring out of your head.

I Have Never Been to Africa

I have never been to Africa –
I've only seen it in my dreams
and longed to go there –
it looked like a giant peach, half-asleep,
gracefully draped in a dried civet-cat skin
someone had sewn small bells and teeth across,
and dancing figures made of ivory
that carry miniature gongs
and miniature hoes –

so no, I've never been to Africa,
and now I just find it embarrassing
to remember sitting in your van
reading MAIN BEAM MAIN BEAM
over and over again, or not even reading it,
but sitting in front of it,
imagining bream, and roach,
flapping lugubriously around our ears
as the van fills up with water;

to remember sitting in your van
trying to impress you
with stories of my travels
that couldn't possibly have been true,
and the van piled high with boxes of shopping,
of hats and coats,
of slinky satin shirts;
boxes of ants
to feed the googling bream.

Fishing

You hang like fruit
on the borders of water and air.
You hang from the night
like a ring from a buffalo's ear.
Right now – which feels like a high-pitched squeal to me –
you're serenely fishing.

They block their airless corridors with flesh,
with cupboards of water,
eyeballs,
lazy days.
Their hearts are the size of pianos,
giant snails.
They file past like butchers with bad breath
on their way to memorial services that last all night.
They presuppose nothing.
They are aloof and unbeholden.
They are loops.
The water is a ballroom for their fins.
You tickle them.

I'm as not-what-you-want
as a squeal-battered piglet at Heathrow;
a breathless telephone call from an escapee
who's finally made it to Chicago,
and who'll have you put inside
if he's found out.
Take absolutely no notice.
Imagine your ears are loops of golden syrup.
Drip them into the lake like liquid gold.
Never speak except the one word *Fishing*.
Never think except the one thought *Fish*.

What the Night Was Made For

Can a very small grandmother,
alone in a room with a pigeon,
learn to fly?

Can a very small grandmother,
even one accustomed to tinkering
with second-hand tractors,
carve up a large man at a wall sink
with the swiftly-rotating discs
of a cement-cutter,
and stow him in eighteen plastic rubbish sacks,
and leave no blood?

And can a very small grandmother
follow the goats around the disused aerodrome,
because she is learning to draw,
and likes their minty eyes and angularity,
without arousing suspicion?

And can a little nun-like daughter like me
be left alone
with a blood-spattered man like you?

And can you tell me
what the night was made for?

Leaving Mother

What do you think I think about, I wonder?
Do you think I think I wish I was your lover?
And what do you think when you think I think like that?

Do you think I think I'd leave the farm and Mother
and hens and cows and woods to live with you?
Or do you think, like me, you must not think?

Think about nothing but nothing,
nothing but *No*, nothing for miles and miles
but *No* on *No*?

My Senior Peacock

My senior peacock with his wall-eyed eyeball's
not so stubborn and superior as you –

why don't you do the not-done thing occasionally,
and encourage *me*
to do the not-done thing you want to do wrong, too?

Such as?
Such as we could go off together somewhere,
just the two of us,
and I could sew you a special sleeper-suit,
and train you to walk backwards
like my bantam;

and we could go out somewhere;
and you wouldn't have to be so serious
and high-minded all the time.
And we could be friends
and talk to one another.

And I wouldn't mind a certain inexperience.
And you wouldn't mind disintegrating hips.

Tomatoes

When I am woken up
by somebody else's lover's
comatose leg on my arm,
cold on the pillow beside me
like a discarded trepanning instrument –

when I am woken up
by a whole string of adjectives
describing my beautiful face –

when I am woken up
by awkward vibrations
disturbing the sweet Georgia air;
by the chandelier starting to drop,
and the balcony collapsing
as I limp out –

when I am woken up
by a lover, or someone dressed as a lover,
elaborately describing their dream –

when my sentences,
instead of flying off like swallows
to distant countries,
lie tangled like spillikins
under the dark hood
of her loved one's plum-coloured eiderdown –

I am about to be made love to
for the first time;
I am about to be crushed
like a bagful of dusty biscuits
under a rolling-pin.

I will get up,
remove a bar of chocolate
from its pile at the back of the fridge,
and walk out into the deserted yard.

I will not notice
the mat of jewels,
the finches,
nor the pleas
that rattle on my head like pure hail.

All I will see is cement,
and the dreamer's placid zebras
having tomatoes hurled against their stripes.

All I will hear is the zoo,
and zoo noises:
caged animals' unseemly
scratches and grunts.

Cattle

I live in a world of bulls and yellow fruit.
I live in a world of sturdy bulls on chains
whose herds of swaying cows are my companions,
their lips and tails and teats
all drooling and warm.

But my obsession with you –
like a speeding car with a knocking exhaust pipe
driven downhill by a party of Whirling Dervishes
with faces like lonely motels –
has upset them.
My obsession –
which goes down on fifty thousand bended knees
and prays for me, like the world's longest monk –
has upset them.

The sponge-cake and the one-eyed swan,
the bell for mass,
the tractor man,
this curious electric typewriter,
soft fruit and yellow flowers,
have been upset:
I live in a world of cows insane with longing.
Mother has made us a pond we can lie down in.

The Winter Pilgrimage

I hear a swarm of bees
making a long winter pilgrimage

across a country where wild flowers
are almost non-existent;

I hear the boy
doing shu-shu in the rushes;

I hear the girl
in the wedding-dress dyed grey;

I hear fish, blood and ice falls,
coloured rains and snows;

but you, though I sprout ears
all over me, like bogs

quivering at night,
I never hear.

The Freezer-Tunnel

Yes, it's a freezer-tunnel!

Say goodbye to the pinks,
and the tall foxgloves,
and the soft-pawed cat
that hunts in the field of sheep;

to delicate sentiments
such as placing flowers
on the tomb of a complete stranger;

to beautiful drawings
found over a long period of time
through searches of the archives
of Swiss mental institutions;

to bees, and important operations
in bee-management;

to the singer who, just as you thought
she was failing, would float
some absolutely ravishing high note;

to the poodle whose owner
carefully lifts her up,
as he too avoids the jellyfish
that's lolling on the beach;

to threshing;
to pig-snouts covered in flies;

and approach it
as an abseiler would,
or an industrial abseiler,
who scales glass:

approach it with your best concentration.

For Days Now I Have Been Imagining It

For days now I have been imagining it:
my taking a deep breath,
my stepping into the room,
your coming slowly towards me
as a lily might –
but what will become of us then,
I want to know:
will it be over?

In spite of our secrets,
as rare and painfully inadequate
as the tadpoles of the forested regions of Borneo;

in spite of our faith,
grim as a mountain range
which we climb and climb,
never to reach the summit,
with its unparalleled views of the surrounding countryside;

in spite of the sheets,
in violet, cerise and mint,
that a nocturnal well-wisher left at the door for us,
will it be over?

And if you think I am going to sit here all afternoon
dreaming about our future,
you're absolutely right:
I'm going to pick you up
like a bridegroom made of sugar on a wedding-cake,
with sugar bones,
and carry you off to the bruised lakes of the future –
with bracelets, cinnamon and shampoo,
we will set up home together on the banks,
just us, and a knee-high moon,
and a few yurts.

B

A Cow Eating Carrots

This ziggurat of putrefying carrots,
the size and shape of an ancient Chevrolet

made of jellied milk and oranges
caramelized on top to make it crunchy,

is how I think of you; I think of me
alternately chewing and drooling, like the cow.

My Italian Cardigan

I owe my Italian cardigan to my cousin;
I owe my new bulb to my aunt;
I owe the death of the black Diamond Rattlesnake
in the shrubbery to Jack;
I owe to a failure of nerve
my well-mannered battery of euphemisms,
which have failed for so long
to call this, this; and that, that; and love, love;
and I owe my sudden, unseemly, quite un-called-for
so-called love,
which is more like You-Know-What,
to You-Know-Who.

Suppose, at the back of an aeroplane,
there was a little balcony
which people could be led to, and sat down on,
and left to themselves in the sky in,
gripping the railings,
to be bumped through the clouds at topspeed
like no one from nowhere to nowhere,
their hearts in their mouths, feeling sick,
but going so fast they can't even go on and *be* sick –
that's like my love,
my feverish love,
for you.

Her Curious Hat

Space is for walking across deserts in,
from dropping into from painted helicopters,
for bleeding in;

space is for sailing ships across,
for listening to,
and being silent in;

space is where tininess goes,
and five thousand years of glass,
and barbecued prawns;

swimming Alsatians,
Van Gogh's baby,
eels;

and Ma,
in her curious silicon rubber hat,
trying to overcome her fear of water.

Where to Fish in Catalonia

If I lie down,
I might feel better;
if I smell the chill
of the almost inaccessible
high-mountain bear-skull sanctuary;
if I feel the silence
of oil poured on oil –

but I just say *speak to me please* –
in a voice as rasping
as a beetle trying vainly to escape
from an increasingly airless jam-jar
embedded in my brain
like a fossilized pistol;
or the silhouettes of jazz-fans
climbing everywhere you look
with huge cases.

If I lie down,
I might feel better.
If I observe the snow,
meet masons,
measure milk;
rub, boil or chip hard seeds
until they germinate;
if I plant forests at will,
I might feel better.
If I study *Where to Fish in Catalonia*,
and dress in silk,
I think I might feel better –

but I never stop inventing
my long intimate conversations with you,
and I never stop missing your van.

If only I were to lie down on the ground
with my head under a blanket
and count fish,
I might feel better,
as they oodle about
in their warm relaxing shoals.

A Small Hotel

My nipples tick
like little bombs of blood.

Someone is walking
in the yard outside.

I don't know why
Our Lord was crucified.

A really good fuck
makes me feel like custard.

Los Cocodrilos de Méjico

Of course I know that I'm not a curled-up shrimp
lost in a world of nothing but snow and ice;
that you're not reading *Los Cocodrilos de Méjico*
because you are a large green creature
with yellow teeth that I can't get out of my head,
but because you like using your brain,
and are learning Spanish;
that you are not an electrician;
that you are not a parakeet;
that you do not provide people in wedding-dresses
with buzzes and squawks like simultaneous orgasms or "peaks";
that you are not walking into town
with a pramful of tulips
to lay at my door;
that the water in the bay is blue and tranquil.
Why else would someone walk into the sea?

The Graceful Giraffe of Clot Bey

When I ascend the terrace steps of Potsdam
between the yew trees clipped to look like polyps,
or a colony of polyps, by cold water,
with no one about on the steps except myself,
having no language but this –
I certainly need you.

When I hear the risen storks,
the cries from whose long coiled throats
can't help sounding mournful,
as if entire courts together with their kings
are slain, dismembered and buried
in valleys that now lie barren –
I certainly need you.

When I say goodbye
with the same dejected air
I imagine Giacometti would wear
if, torn from his work
and his beautiful brother Diego,
he was set on the deck of a ship
bound for an island inhabited by nothing but tortoises
lumbering about on volcanoes
like abandoned radiators;

when I wave
like sallow mutants discarding limbs
in twilit marshland settlements
where only the rats survive;

when my eyes blur,
like the graceful giraffe's of Clot Bey
who continued to gladden the hearts of Parisians
for sixteen years before she died,
mute and majestic,
sunk on her bed of straw –
I certainly need you.

When the telephone,
like a bricked-up cathedral,
refuses to ring;
like a one-hundred-fingered ice-encrusted orchestra,
primed,
beribboned,
and triumphant,
which refuses to strike up and play
without its seraphic conductor –
I certainly need you.

Baby clams wilt in yellow brine.
Van Gogh's ear wilts in a jar in a police station.
My heart, equally forsaken,
wilts in the screw-top jar of your not coming.

Coition

You'll have to lie perfectly still
like a nude with a rat;

and when I have finished,
you'll have not a hair on your head,

and everyone else in the world
will have gone to sleep.

Peafowl

Forty desultory peafowl, raised by me,
are posing on my milk-crates,
cupboards,
crutches,
taps
and enemas.

When people die,
one sees them playing croquet,
singing,
weaving:
In my case, I'll be someone one avoids –
being screeched at by, and screeching at, vain peafowl.

What Do I Really Believe?

I believe that Benedictine
tastes like a meteor;

I believe that antitheses and hyperboles
dilate like slowly eaten fruit;

I believe that when a man takes long, deep breaths
he is trying not to prematurely ejaculate;

that tangerines are oranges, and full of juice,
and do not move unless they are being carried;

that the idea of repelling the rabbits
with moth flakes was not a success;

that abbatoirs binge
on Santa Gertrudis bulls;

that if I meet someone I like,
I start to do it unconsciously;

that a prisoner is painting the bars of his cell sky-blue,
and a tall giraffe is living in a summer-house in Maine;

that Beethoven was so deaf
he thought he was a painter;

that giant slugs
can be bigger than chihuahuas;

that I always seem to get
the wrong end of the stick;

that I love you very much,
but it doesn't seem to make the slightest difference;

that it's all very well
but why don't you love me too?

that there ought to be a law against chihuahuas,
that no one has to groom a giant slug.

The Bed

This is the bed
that I became a woman in,
that I lay naked on on tepid nights,
after my grandmother's scaly-fingered gardener
half-marched, half crept in here and mended it
(like a man mends a cage in a zoo,
with excited reluctance);
I lay in the shade
of this lop-sided wardrobe –
that looks like a caramelized ungainly antelope
with nothing between its head and the constellations
except the occasional stiff-winged aeroplane –

and sent my long gold clitoris to sea
between my legs, streamlined and sweet
like a barge
laden with sweetmeats and monkeys
bound for some distant land;
and this is the bed I saw the chickens from,
running across the yard without their heads,
and smelt the farmers
leaning on their cows that had cars' names –
a smell of blood and milking and desire
I was suddenly part of, and sunk in,
like necks in Startena.

Toy Aeroplanes

I have decided to get on quietly with my work
and not think about you any more.
I'll be like the Dalai Lama painting aeroplanes,

row upon row, and never getting distracted.
Topaz? Egg? Canaries? Tanzania?
What's the yellowest thing you can imagine?

Because that's the colour I think of my love for you as;
or the colour of those crazy little dogs, do you remember,
who didn't have a clue what they were supposed to be doing?

Hippos

Glistening hippos float about like chocolate
bumping into everything. They're you.
I don't know what's come over me.
I do. For three days now
I've been on the straight and narrow.
I come indoors. To what?
To thoughts of you: veiled hippopotami,
trying to be invisible, romping
with their eyes closed in my bedroom.

Much Against Everyone's Advice

Much against everyone's advice,
I have decided I must not be put off any longer
from coming into the yard
and telling you the truth, as best I can.
There's something I've got to tell you I will say.
Yes, I have been practising, you see –
you would be proud of me.
Alone in this ridiculous café,
with stiffened hair,
holding your last letter
like a penitent teenager
stranded on a cliff
who clutches the Bible
thank God she remembered to bring,
I have been practising.

Do you remember the boat
that dropped from the sky
right into Granma's garden,
just as two little girls,
never to visit fairyland again,
strayed out of the pecan grove?
And Granma turned over in her sleep
and saw a blond young pilot
who looked like Jesus
gazing into her eyes
from just about the level of her bedroom window?
Who ran his hands backwards and forwards
along his glossy cockpit
as if it were a prize bull
and not a stunted machine
that had ruined our lives forever;
who looked down at the boat
as if she were a dancer, in perfect order,
and not a boat
creaking among squashed roses in our border?

All year he had been practising for this,
and I have too.
Much against everyone's advice,
I have decided to tell you everything
– poor worm.

Cow

I want to be a cow
and not my mother's daughter.
I want to be a cow
and not in love with you.
I want to feel free to feel calm.
I want to be a cow who never knows
the kind of love you 'fall in love with' with;
a queenly cow, with hips as big and sound
as a department store,
a cow the farmer milks on bended knee,
who when she dies will feel dawn
bending over her like lawn to wet her lips.

I want to be a cow,
nothing fancy –
a cargo of grass,
a hammock of soupy milk
whose floating and rocking and dribbling's undisturbed
by the echo of hooves to the city;
of crunching boots;
of suspicious-looking trailers parked on verges;
of unscrupulous restaurant-owners
who stumble, pink-eyed, from stale beds
into a world of lobsters and warm telephones;
of streamlined Japanese freighters
ironing the night,
heavy with sweet desire like bowls of jam.

The Tibetans have 85 words for states of consciousness.
This dozy cow I want to be has none.
She doesn't speak.
She doesn't do housework or worry about her appearance.
She doesn't roam.
Safe in her fleet
of shorn-white-bowl-like friends,
she needs, and loves, and's loved by,
only this –
the farm I want to be a cow on too.

Don't come looking for me.
Don't come walking out into the bright sunlight
looking for me,
black in your gloves and stockings and sleeves
and large hat.
Don't call the tractorman.
Don't call the neighbours.
Don't make a special fruit-cake for when I come home:
I'm not coming home.
I'm going to be a cowman's counted cow.
I'm going to be a cow
and you won't know me.

The Convent of Sleep

If you are a good, calm person,
you join the convent of sleep
and are heard from no more for the rest of the night;
but if you are a worrier and fantasiser,
you roam about the borders of your dream-world
getting into all sorts of trouble,
and drawing the wrath of people
who don't believe in anything that makes sense,
and are full of secrets and irregularities,
down on your head like a hood.

Think of the pain.
Think of the silence.
Think of the silence aboard the Mignonette
after the two crew members killed and ate the cabin boy;
think of their mothers
falling in love with their fathers;
think of the pain of falling in love,
and don't.
Just sleep good clean hard sleeps
like white potatoes rolling down the middle of the night.

This Afternoon I Swallowed a Cornfield

This afternoon I swallowed a cornfield,
and three painted water-towers
and a pecan grove,
and a gravel pit I'd never seen before,
and the warm creamy lake at the bottom of it,
and the panama hat
that was quietly circling around it,
and the little man who suddenly sprang up
and ran away towards a deserted railway station
and stepped into a carriage
without looking back,
but whose face –
in spite of the heat,
in spite of my being half-dizzy
beside where a cornfield was,
in spite of my trying to fail to remember who you are –
whose face,
like a deer that's no more than the thought of a deer,
no more than a wish in the air,
was unquestionably yours.
That's what I do.
I swallow things.
I lie and dream and sweat and swallow things.

I Want to Run Away

I want to run away into the woods;
to kill weasels in wheat silos;
to live in the woods,
with my disfigured face exposed,
without a name;
to stay in the woods
until I belong to the woods –
and if somebody finds me alive,
and they may,
they'll shoot.
Ma will have said she's a liar, and armed,
and to shoot.

I heard of a mother once
who kept her daughter
under the floorboards: *Mother,*
do it to me please. Mother, do it to me.
When I'm not being me being me,
but just being dumb,
she likes it.
And the more half-witted I am,
the more she likes it.
Stuff me under the floorboards. Crack my knees.
And if I am not to your liking,
shoot me please.

Crossing the Desert in a Pram

And when my ears fill up with sand,
and everything goes quiet,

lie down in the hood with me.
Pretend the sand is fur.

They'll find us with a little beeping tube
that finds rare animals. They think I am a shoe.

The leader of the expedition
can't believe his luck.

He waves the shoe about above his head...
Relax, I hear her say, *my dear, relax.*

Twenty Little Monks

But Sister, I can't. I can't.
It keeps coming back.
Like an ice-decked, brain-damaged bear
that stumbles out of the forest,
alternately growling and tinkling,
it keeps coming back. And I can't.

Rangers keep coming back;
busloads of mothers
keep coming back;
and soldiers with blue eyes
camping on the hillside
like hydrangeas;
meat-eating, weaponry,
and abattoirs;
rumours about castrati;
yellow hens.
Somebody's jealous.
Somebody's certainly not.
Speak to me, somebody whispers
Speak to me please.

And twenty little monks
start turning in my head,
twenty little monks
in skirts and cardigans,
shorn and fragrant,
dancing in the snow.

Daily Prudence

Eternity begins in time,
and we must stop thinking about it
as something that follows time.
Eternity is in Startena,
figs,
and distant waders.
Eternity is in the man selling posts,
in lapel-pins,
in W.C. Fields on the new television set
Sister Evangelist's sent;

and, above all, Eternity begins in,
and is not repudiated by,
and flowers like the Lady Bankshire roses in,
something I need right now,
regarding you –
(don't mention the thought of you) –
I mean in prudence.
Sandbags
to stop the whole cascade of degeneration in the brain;
well-crafted moats;
still water;
missals:
prudence.
Something all daughters are taught
by all good mothers:
the still, well-crafted moats
of daily
prudence.

What Are Fields For?

What are fields for?
To go long-jumping with you and Thomas Merton on.
What is scaffolding for?
To see the tiny buildings below us from.
What are sheets for?
To be wrapped up with you all night in.
And what is this longing for?
And why is it always you I'm thinking of?
I think of you.
Why you?
It's always you.
You're eating tomato ice-cream with a long spoon.
You're copying out the entire Bible by hand,
book by book.
You're dismantling scaffolding.
You're hiking with a mattress in the rain.
You're abandoning a naked baby
on the front steps of an Old People's Home.
You're frying my one-legged pea-chick.
You're at a station.
And I say to myself 'Say *Make yourself numb* to yourself.
Say *Make yourself make yourself numb*.
Say *Take no notice*.
Trample on his arms and legs and universe
like someone trampling on the arms and legs
of bodies washed up on a beach
with bits of string and grapefruit and dead fish.'
I say all sorts of things.
It makes no difference.
I think of you.
It's you.
It's always you.
That's what they're there for,
it's for, he's for, I'm for, we're for
– always you.

Desire's a Desire

It taunts me
like the muzzle of a gun;
it sinks into my soul like chilled honey
packed into the depths of treacherous wounds;
it wraps me up in cold green sheets
like Indian squaws
who wrap their babies in the soft green sheathes of irises
that smell of starch;
it tattooes my shins;
it itches my thighs
like rampant vaginal flora;
it tickles my cheeks
like silkworms munching mulberry leaves
on silk farms;
it nuzzles my plucked armpits like fat dogs;
it plays me
like a piano being played
by regimented fingers
through pressed sheets;
it walks across my back
like geese at dawn,
or the gentle manners
of my only nurse,
who handles me like glass, or Bethlehem.

My skin is white.
I neither eat nor sleep.
My only desire's a desire
to be free from desire.

Do It Again

I like the feeling.
Do it again.
No, don't.
It ripples like the soft fur of the tapir
of rhinoceros-family fame,
that feeds on sprouts;
or the rug I smuggled three live ducks for Mother in
on Eastern Airways;

but all we're allowed's anxiety like fishbones
lodged in our throats
as beauty parlours hum;
all we're allowed is having pretty faces
and cold and glittery hearts like water-ices.
Mine's more like a centrally-heated boiler-room,
evil and warm;
like kidneys on a plate.

But all we're allowed's the dry hum of the driers;
all we're allowed's one word,
like darkness:
No.

Me

If the man mending fences
had seen a big familiar girl with bloodshot eyes
heading across the pasture
towards the woods;
if her skin was yellow and blotched,
and something was wrong with her legs;

and if she was being squawked at
by a flock of turkeys,
a pen of pheasants,
and a pen of quails;
by a retinue of abandoned peacocks
from a cedar tree,
who have travelled in a crate
all the way from a Florida orange grove
to a Georgia cattle farm,
only to be walked out on again;
whose Mother was yelling *Where the hell has she gone?*
it was me.

And where was I going,
and why was I going there,
my heart like a sump,
to the woods of the hawk and the fox,
the opossum and snake,
to sunsets playing like organs,
stubborn
and radiant?
You.

I Want To Be Alone

I want to be alone with my duck,
who won the hearts of the nation's good-natured women
with his little irregular snuffles
like mice in bags
as I wheeled him round the lakes
in his sprung pram;
and with my goose,
out hiking in the rain again
among small cattle;
and you, my swan, with your fine taste in snow-white linens.

I want to be alone with my quails.
I want to be alone with my Startena.
I want to be alone with Calomel.
I want to be alone with the Sword
that cuts, that Christ has said He came to bring.

What Do I Really Want

My one-legged, mown-down peacock,
Limpy's sleepy.

Memories of you
are sleepy too.

What do I really want?
Bejewelled jodhpurs?

Peace of mind
is the correct answer.

Sister

Peace of mind is the correct answer.
National Chicken Week is the correct answer.
Roy Rogers' horse attending a church service
in Pasadena is the correct answer;
Banjo, my cherry-red Santa Gertrudis bull with big white eyes
and chubby lips, is the correct answer;
Barred Rockfryers is the correct answer;
their expression of alert composure
is the correct answer;
Equinox, the jackass, is the correct answer;
Lady Bankshire and Herbert Hoover roses
is the correct answer;
Thomas Merton is the correct answer;
The Body of Christ
is the correct answer;
The Instrument of Crucifixion
is the correct answer;
Mother, like butter, is surely the correct answer;
Sister, the Muscovy duck, is the correct answer,
as she flaps consolingly past our living-room window –
Mother's ex-Trappist-Monastery, tough, Trappist-monk of a duck.